SECRETS of WISDOM from MOTHER'S HEART

JOE ALDRICH

CONTENTS

*D*uring my senior year in high school my mother, Doris Coffin Aldrich, was killed in an automobile accident. Mother was an extremely intelligent, highly educated woman. She studied at the University of Washington and graduated from Biola College. Married at thirty-one to Willard Aldrich (the President of Multnomah Bible College and Biblical Seminary for thirty-five years), she bore nine children. Her clearly stated mission was to raise a godly family.

As Mom's life so clearly demonstrated, the high and holy calling of motherhood is one of the most challenging assignments on the face of the earth. It is a sacred trust, a commitment to use every means possible to help each child grow up loving Jesus and embracing His agenda for life.

Foreword

A godly mother counteracts the influences of contemporary culture by structuring an environment where beauty reigns. Our threadbare sofas, sagging springs, and frayed carpets did not deter us from the beauty of God's handiwork that surrounded us. Although well-used, our home was truly that—a home, not a house. Sweaty, sloppy boys fought with glee in it. Oil leaked from the oil-stove, bathtubs overflowed, food frequently ended up on the floor, tricycles clogged doorways or blocked traffic in the kitchen. More often than not, beds were left unmade. Most mornings there were wet sheets and pajamas to attend to, not to mention all the other clothes that needed to be washed and washed and washed again.

But in the midst of what I'm sure seemed like chaos, there was beauty.

Our family orchestra "made a joyful noise."

Our family read the Word of God daily.

We prayed together at meals, and Mom or Dad prayed with each of us at bedtime.

We celebrated birthdays with gusto.

Our imaginations and spirits were expanded by the host of Christian leaders Mother entertained.

Mom and Dad decided not to have a TV in the house; we subscribed to over a dozen good, wholesome magazines.

All of this contributed to an atmosphere, an environment filled with the music of the gospel. This was not an accident. My parents intentionally chose to make the godliness of their children of highest priority.

Mom determined to know the bent of each of us and to plant seeds that challenged us according to our abilities. She was a great coach. She believed in each of her "players" and sought God's best for each one with much prayer. And her positive reinforcement worked. Today all three of my brothers are in full-time ministry, three of my five sisters are married to ministers, and we all have a vital relationship with the Lord. To God be the glory!

Our dear mother never learned to drive, yet she spoke over fifty times a year to every imaginable audience. In her "spare time," Mom wrote a monthly column for Moody magazine called "Out of the Mixing Bowl," which was read by thousands of women over a period of eighteen years.

This book is a collection of some of the more than 300 articles that Mother wrote. Each is self-contained, developing a basic idea that grew out of a vast array of experiences and events on our small farm just north of Portland—Aldrich Acres.

Along with Mom's writings, I have included some of my own thoughts and reflections from my childhood. I think you will find these pages filled with warm and loving thoughts, wisdom, and insight that will inspire you to be all that God wants you to be.

Come along with me as I look back with great fondness and deep love on the life of a remarkable woman—my mother, Doris Coffin Aldrich.

JOE ALDRICH
November, 1998

Spicy cinnamon, shortening, and fat brown eggs are not all that go into the big blue mixing bowl.

Womenfolk are busy, especially mothers with three small children, and there isn't time for quiet-handed meditation. Many a problem is thought through over the mixing bowl and many a prayer is raised even as the ingredients for the cake are measured out. Even then the heart may be lifted to the Lord as one problem and then another comes to mind. It isn't always problems —sometimes a bit of

A Quiet Place Within My Heart

fellowship with the Lord as we rejoice in His lovingkindness. And we tell Him:

"My hands must needs be busy, Lord. My day is full—too full for any length of time alone with Thee. In the midst of all the busyness, keep within my heart a quiet place, and let me learn of Thy sufficiency."

A Thought from Joe

I t was June 25, 1941 when Mother wrote her first monthly letter, "Out of the Mixing Bowl," which she continued to write and distribute to hundreds of women until 1958. I was her chubby, seven-month-old baby, Jon was a year and a half, and Jane was pushing three. Mother described us as her "Three Jays."

She said *"my hands must needs be busy, Lord,"* and indeed her hands were! Washing, ironing, cooking, feeding, bathing, correcting, cleaning, chauffeuring, and shopping.

Our lives are not much different today. Sometimes we must confess what God already knows: there isn't time for quiet-handed meditation. So like mother we pray *"In the midst of busyness, keep within my heart a quiet place."*

Hands in the dishwater . . . talking with God.
Folding clothes . . . talking with God.
Waiting on the phone . . . talking with God.
Driving the car . . . talking with God.

Busy hands *and* a quiet heart!

F ive lines of clothes of a Monday morning and a brisk wind blowing them dry. Over there in the garden the bush beans about ready for picking, and the row of sunflowers stretching to the sun. Summertime—and one made glad by God's lovingkindness.

The mind likes to toy with a word, turning it, trying it this way and that until the fullness of meaning is more fully realized. . . . The word, *lovingkindness* is found in numerous passages [of Scripture].

Lovingkindness

Let us dwell on it a moment—there is *kindness*—there is more, there is *loving-kindness*. We mull that over. Is every kindness not loving? Does it not sometimes spring from a sense of duty and not from love as its source? Is there a kindness that even while it acts, looks with a measure of coolness upon its object?

But what of lovingkindness? There is warmth there, and shelter. The hesitant, weary child of God may confidently turn and rest in lovingkindness.

A THOUGHT FROM JOE

Is there anything more delicious than clean sheets dried in the sun of an August morn? But when the sun turned to rain, the sheets had to be hung from a clothesline in the basement. All the soggy wash found its way to the line and stayed there as long as the clothespins held.

Lovingkindness can be a new automatic dryer. I remember when mamma got her first one. The sheets no longer smelled like newly mowed hay, but the workload for mamma—with a family of eleven—was cut down significantly. God supplied that dryer for us. His provision was truly lovingkindness.

Isn't it encouraging to know that God's acts of kindness are driven by His heart of love? While kindness may produce helpful actions out of a sense of duty, love acts because the lover delights in the object of his love. We are the object of God's love.

D own on my knees in the carrot bed and time for a bit of thinking—the baby on a blanket between the rows, kicking brown chubby legs in the warm sunshine— weeding . . . and weeds.

The roots of couch grass grow deep and strong and with great determination. Couch grass can't be reasoned with nor treated gently—it must be rooted out. . . . Drastic measures are called for.

Rooting Out Sin

Sin is like couch grass. It runs deep and strong in the human heart, and programs of outward reformation do not touch the roots. A man cannot lift himself by his own bootstraps. No more can he rid his heart of sin. Who, then, can help us? The Lord Jesus Christ, our Savior, who is "mighty to save." . . .

How we need to keep the garden of our hearts free from the sins that spring up there—that flash of temper, the bit of pride, the covetous spirit.

A THOUGHT FROM JOE

I hate pig weeds. I'm not sure of their botanical name, we just called them "pig weeds." Next to the rock pile, pulling pig weeds in the garden was the worse place to be exiled in the Aldrich domain. I'd rather clean out the loafing shed, change the irrigation pipes, or mend fences. But if you didn't root them out while they were little and the soil was damp, you wouldn't get them.

Three important doctrines illustrate how sin can be rooted out of our lives.

Justification: The moment we turn from self and all self-effort and embrace Christ as our Savior, we are declared righteous. Christ paid the penalty for our sins when He died on the cross.

Sanctification: This is a process of being delivered daily from the power of sin, by exercising spiritual disciplines.

Glorification: One day we will be delivered from the very presence of sin. Jesus is coming again to take us to a place where there is no more pig weed!

Hurrying up the basement stairs with a jar of applesauce for breakfast, I arrived at the kitchen door just in time to see Jon quickly replace the cover on the sugar bowl.

To my, "Oh Jon!" he smiled blandly and cheerily replied, "Just lookin', Mom."

When the offender is two-and-a-half, we smile to

Just Lookin'

ourselves at the little rascal. But when an adult is "just lookin" at the forbidden thing, we feel concern. . . .

How we need to thank the Lord for the times He has checked us when we were "just lookin'," and how we need to pray for a heart responsive to His admonition. Remember Lot who looked too long and the sorrow it brought to him!

Yes, Jon boy, you can teach your Mommy lots of things while she's working around the kitchen—and may she have the grace to learn.

One of the chores of winter was pruning the orchard. The cut-off limbs were carried to a burning spot and set on fire. My self-assigned task was to feed the fire—when I was all of three years old—and Mom always kept her eyes on me. When she saw me getting too close to the fire she would bang on the window and motion me away from it. I got caught "just lookin'" several times.

"Just lookin'" can be the first step towards sin.

The Lord saw Eve when she was *just lookin'*.

The Lord saw Lot's wife when she was *just lookin'*.

The Lord saw David when he was *just lookin'*.

Thank the Lord, He will never give up banging the window and motioning us away from the things that would harm us.

There on the kitchen window ledge, we have four pressed-glass doll dishes that used to belong to "Mommie" when she was a little girl. The light shines through them and lends a sparkle to the room. On gray days they are a comfort to one's soul!

In order to keep them sparkling, they need a frequent

This Little Light of Mine

washing in good, hot soapy water. So into the dishpan they go, those little sugar bowls and cream-pitchers and out they come to shine again. And all the time they are shining, they have a lesson to teach.

If the light of the knowledge of the Lord is to shine through us, we need to be clean.

One is reminded of the little girl who wondered what a saint might be. One day she was taken to view the priceless stained-glass windows of a great cathedral. There in the beauty and quietness, she exclaimed, "Now I know what saints are. They are people who let the light shine through."

Oh lovely Lord, may our lives not hinder Thy beauty from shining through!

God's communication strategy is to wrap ideas in people. That's the key to communicating the gospel. Authentic, caring, serving, giving folks who play the music of the gospel. Many people have heard the words, but very few have heard the music or seen the sparkle.

Our mission is to make visible the invisible God, to be living epistles, shining stars, fragrant aromas, salt and light, a gracious servant.

The prophet Isaiah says,

"Your light will break forth like the dawn . . .

if you share your food with the hungry,

provide the poor wanderer with shelter,

and clothe the naked." (Is. 58:8-10)

Saints are people who let the light shine through.

Sometimes we cut our gingersnaps with a heart-shaped cookie cutter. Jane has her own small rolling pin, and her little hands labor over the sticky dough.

"We are busy people, aren't we Mommie? Why do we make heart cookies?"

Sometimes we pack a box of cookies and send them to someone we love. We are sure to include some hearts in with the stars,

A Place in God's Heart

the bunnies, and the round cookies.

February is the month of hearts, of warmth of sentiment, of love. One is reminded of a poem by an unknown author.

I gave father a Valentine
It had his name in a heart with mine;
It had my name in a heart with his,
And three silver cupids blowing a kiss.
He was surprised at the cupid part,
But he said he was used to my name in his heart.

Author Unknown

God has your name in His heart. . . . Do you have *His* name in your heart?

A THOUGHT FROM JOE

To receive a heart-shaped cookie from the One who said, "Let not your heart be troubled," may seem a bit incongruous, but didn't God's chosen people eat manna from heaven? And wasn't Elijah fed by divinely directed ravens?

God said, "Let not your heart be troubled." Why? Because you've got a special place in His heart. Not because of anything you did. He loves you in spite of what you've done. No one is beyond the grace of God. Once you respond to God's free gift of salvation, you are reconciled to Him forever.

March, the stormy month, when silver rain slants down at us and the wind rushes by on business of his own. Indoors, the mixing-bowl turns out raised cinnamon rolls, chock full of puffy raisins and sweet with syrupy brown sugar.

A Shelter from the Storm

The fragrance and warmth indoors contrast with the cold storms outside and serve to help define security and home.

It's a stormy time in the world today. Thousands are homeless—out in the cold. Is there any place of shelter for them? There is heart-shelter in the Lord Jesus Christ of whom it is written,

"And a man [Jesus] shall be as an hiding place from the wind, a shelter from the tempest."

Bodily shelter may yet be denied to all of us, but our hearts can be sheltered snug in Him, the God of all grace and comforts.

A THOUGHT FROM JOE

O ur lives seem to be a pilgrimage between the cold
storms outside and warmth on the inside. We travel
between seasons of success and failure, expectation and
disappointment, fear and hope.

The rooster and hens at Aldrich Acres knew the security of
the rafters in the barn. As darkness fell they meandered into it
and flew up into the rafters, which proved to be a haven from
marauding foxes and skunks. They would visit for a while and
soon be sound asleep, oblivious to the tempest outside.

The cows tagged the loafing shed for their shelter in the
time of storm. Out of the mud and rain, they settled down to
munch on hay without a care in the world. Often my "haven of
rest" was that old red barn. With darkness around me, the
wind screeching, and the timbers groaning, I sometimes
found myself sitting alone in the haymow listening to the
peaceful sound of the contented cows munching hay.

The God who feeds the cows, takes care of the chickens,
and feeds the sparrows specializes in security. He is our rock,
our fortress, our strong tower, our Father, and our God. He is
our shelter in the time of storm.

Wisdom from

Mother's

Heart

J ust outside our kitchen window there is a lilac bush and the new green leaves are beginning to bud. April is the month of unfolding life, full of promise for spring and summer. It's a pleasure to work in the kitchen and look out at the growing loveliness.

Children Are Growing Things

The new leaves and buds are tender things, but they grow to sturdiness and strength if not injured. . . . The little children entrusted to our care—they too will grow in the knowledge of the Lord if not injured.

And may they come to a fullness of understanding of their need of Him as Savior. And may we help them in their growing years to see the Lord as the "altogether lovely one" who loved us and gave Himself for us.

April, and growing things . . . our children and their need of a Savior. Lord make us faithful in living before them.

A THOUGHT FROM JOE

Like April's fragile buds, children are planted in environments that may or may not support healthy growth. They become like the people they associate with. If these little "buds" are going to survive the storm and avoid the pestilence, they need strong role models committed to raising them within the boundary conditions of God's character. They need to know God's rules, yet they have an incredible ability to close their ears to advice and open their eyes to example.

Our children need to know Jesus as their personal Savior. May we be faithful to live Him before them.

It was Jane's fourth birthday and to celebrate we went over to Portland and bought her very first pair of shiny black patent-leather slippers. Then we went to Meier & Frank's and had ice cream. Jane had "pink" and Mommie had chocolate, and Jane's big eyes were a-shine with gladness and Mommie's heart was warm around the cockles.

Friendship and Fellowship

What was the special satisfaction? Was it that she was my child?

No—it was that my child was getting old enough for fellow-ship, for sharing experiences together.

She looked cunning perched upon the high stool, busy with her ice cream and quick peeks at her thrust-out, slippered foot, and ever so often a smile that said: "We're having fun together." . . .

[Perhaps] our joy in the Lord [would] be more full and His delight in us more satisfying to His heart, if we had more of a feeling of "togetherness" in our daily walk with Him. Are we growing in our knowledge of the Lord and our enjoyment of Him?

It's the fellowship that makes the difference and the delight, to our heart . . . and His.

M an's chief aim," according to the Westminster Confession, "is to glorify God and enjoy Him forever." So how do we glorify God? We glorify God by enjoying Him forever.

Often the Lord encouraged His followers to "lift up their eyes and look." The star-studded skies declare the glory of the Lord; the earth teems with evidence of His creative genius.

The cry of a loon, the coyote chorus, the melodic music of the song birds, the dissonance of the crow, the coo of the dove . . . all these and more are signposts pointing to a personal God who gives marvelous gifts to His children—to enjoy.

If God has given us all things richly to enjoy isn't it about time we started glorifying God by enjoying what He has given?

So Far Down and So Heavy

We were making biscuits, and Jane was rolling and re-rolling the scraps into dubious creations of delicate gray. Once again she raised the question, "But Mommie, how will we get to heaven?"

She paused in her work, her be-floured little face all intent on the answer. To the assurance that the Lord would see to it for us, she replied, "But Mommie, it's so far down and you're so heavy."

Underneath the laughter there is the sobering fact of the spiritual realities. "So far down". . . it tears your heart to think how far down it was for [Christ] to come from the glory of heaven to the sin of earth.

Far down, but He came because His love compelled Him. "And you're so heavy." Yes, the weight of all my sin was laid upon Him. . . .

Yes, He can get us to Heaven, because He came so far down and He bore so heavy a weight of sin. "For God so loved the world that He gave His only begotten Son, that whoever believes in Him should not perish but have everlasting life" (John 3:16).

I t can be healthy to remind ourselves every now and then just how far down Christ came to lift from us the heaviness of our sin. We must never make light of the holiness of God and the awfulness of sin. Have you ever observed that the longer you walk with the Lord the "heavier" your sin feels? That's as it should be, for as we grow in understanding of God's absolute holiness, we find ourselves crying out like Isaiah, "Woe is me, for I am undone! . . . For my eyes have seen the King, the LORD of hosts" (Isa. 6:5).

Then there are times when Satan tries to lead us on archaeological expeditions into our past, inviting us to sort through the refuse and junk. Of course he never reminds us that God has stamped "paid in full" across our account and posted our past "off limits"!

No matter how far down we are or how "heavy" our sins, Christ gives His love and forgiveness freely to all who ask.

Who Will Care for Us?

Daddy had to go away on a trip, and Daddy was missed. A slightly damp and very dejected little trio stood in the middle of the living room the next morning. . . .

"Where Daddy?" demanded Jon, and Joe's dark eyes looked straight at Mommie for the answer. "Daddy has gone to Wenatchee for a few days. He'll be home pretty soon to see you."

"Who will take care of us?" queried Jane, her eyes filling with tears.

"Well, honey, Mommie will take care of you."

For a moment she was satisfied, and then in a rush of tears she cried, "But Mommie, who will take care of you?" She was quieted when Mother explained that the Lord Jesus would take care of us all, because He never has to go away on trips . . . .

There are many homes today from which "Daddy" has gone. . . . Those who know the Lord experience the "peace that passes understanding."

And to those who do not yet know Him, the invitation still stands. "Come to Me, all you who labor and are heavy laden, and I will give you rest" (Matt. 11:28).

When dads aren't around, children face questions about their own security. With Dad absent, who will protect them from harm? Who will provide food, clothing, and shelter? Who will be their special friend?

"Mommie will take care of you."

And moms of every size, description, and race have done just that. Nothing can compare with a mother's caring, nurturing aptitude. I'm certain children are helped by assurances that Mom will be there, that she will be their source of security and strength, that she will stand between them and a hostile world.

But *who will take care of* Mommie?—a faithful, heavenly Father who never leaves, never forsakes, never fails. One who delights in His children, He is a friend who listens, cares, and responds. He is also a father to the fatherless. He understands the pain and hurt when families come apart, when dads and moms look for greener pastures, when children face the consequences of a divided home, of fractured relationships.

And He is *always* there.

Jesus' Birthday

We were talking about Christmas the other day and reminding ourselves again that it was the Lord Jesus' birthday. "I'll give him a wiggle-bug," said Jon. Jane added, "And I'll give Him a bag of candy and a flower for His house. Would He love me for that, Mommie?" How can one explain to a wee girlie that He loves us not for what we give to Him but for what we *are* to Him? . . . It was prayer time, and Mommie prayed, "We thank Thee, dear Lord, for Christmas and all the joy it will bring." Jane broke in with, "And that it's the Lord Jesus' birthday and that we love Him and that I will climb in His lap and put my arms around Him and love Him." Unorthodox perhaps, and yet it must be that sort of statement which warms His heart.

After all, more than all the Christmas shopping, decorating, programs, and rush—much of it in His honor— more precious than all that to Him is the quiet place within our hearts where we say, "Christmas . . . His birthday . . . I love Him."

Thе Christmas season was always a special time for the Aldrich clan. Mom went all out to make it a memorable occasion. On Christmas morning four bright-eyed youngsters whooped it up around the tree decorated with strings of popcorn, colored paper cut-outs, and "silver rain" unevenly distributed around its boughs. What captured the frolicking foursome, however, was not the beauty of the tree, but the bounty of gifts stashed underneath.

Since we were too young for carols, Mom would start off with some well-known tune like "Jesus Loves Me." The versions differed. Joe droned "Jesus loves me, I don't know." Afterward there were prayers of thankfulness. It was a familiar ritual for Mom and Dad to lead us in thanking God for His great gift to mankind . . . His Son, Jesus Christ.

Jane wanted to give Him *a bag of candy and a flower for His house*. His Father-heart would be moved by that. But wonder of it all . . . He invites us to bring all our heartaches, failures, and rebellion to the foot of the cross. And there we find no condemnation but peace with God.

He gives and gives and gives again. It's Christmas every day.

The Father of Lights from
heaven above,
Guided the Eastern Star;
He drew with its light to the
Son of His love
Wise men from lands afar.

The light of the star led
men to see
The Babe in the manger bed;
A King they saw who'd set
them free,
And reign in David's stead.

The Father's heart with joy
looked down,
Yet suffered infinite loss;
He saw the King they've
yet to crown
Born in the shadow of
the cross.

WILLARD ALDRICH

God Knows the Recipe

A bit of spice, the basic flour, the shortening and the milk, the leavening and the salt, the sugar and the eggs—combine to form that final |birthday cake| which we later serve with pride. The ingredients are not all tasty but all are needed, and the sifting and stirring as well as the heat of the oven are all necessary.

Every so often throughout the year there comes a day with special zest . . . a bit of spice. And then perhaps a whole week of the weariness of the daily round—just some flour perhaps—and not very interesting, but nourishing and a part of the whole. And the sweetness of some days—how we wish it could last, and yet you know what happens when too much sugar goes into a recipe . . . it falls flat.

And what of the times when the heart is so heavy it feels like a weight? Leaven is bitter to the taste, and yet no cake will achieve perfection without it. And the One who knows the recipe-of-the-year for us never uses too much leavening lest the cake be bitter. He balances and combines it all with understanding skill. He does this for those who let Him. . . .

|A year| is more than just 365 days. Somehow there's a recipe and it all works together.

A THOUGHT FROM JOE

Mother wrote this poem when she was just a young girl of sixteen. I think it fits well here with her thoughts about the new year that lay ahead.

The New Day

A lovely glorious new day
Which God has given me.
I hold thee in my cupped
    hands,
Carefully and eagerly.

So new, so clean, so free
    from stain,
As yet no spot of sin.
I dare not trust myself
    with thee,
So give thee back to Him.

DORIS COFFIN

Love in an Orange Wrapper

It was only a fence-staple, wrapped in a crumpled Sunkist orange wrapper and tied with a piece of dirty string, yet it had its place close by the white frosted birthday-cake with its red candies and blue crepe-paper bows. It was *more* than a fence-staple—it was Jon's birthday gift to his daddy, and it was received with all the honor due the loving little heart which labored over the difficult task of wrapping it. And so it held its place among the gifts much more grand and costly.

There among the offerings given to the Lord lies one so small and poor that surely it would not be noticed. Sometimes its very poorness makes it stand out from the more pretentious gifts, and we may be sure that the great heart of love whose eye is quick to note every love-token, will see and rejoice in the gift. . . .

After all, of what does He stand in need? Is He not the great Creator of Heaven and Earth? And will our puny little gift make much difference to Him? Not the gift itself, perhaps, but the heart behind it—well, that means more to Him than all the world beside. Love sees beyond the self . . . and understands.

Brother Jon was thinking of dad, but how he came up with a staple I'll never know. You don't buy staples at a gift-shop. Staples are neither expensive nor attractive. They're usually sold by the pound at hardware stores. Find the nail bins and you're close to the staples.

Whatever the source of the staple, whatever his expectation, Jon apparently anticipated that, meager as his gift might be, dad would be delighted—and so he was.

Dad saw the dirty string, the orange wrapper, the single staple. Dad saw Jon's eager little face. Dad saw a tender heart. Dad made a little boy's day. He smiled, he hugged, he thanked, he was pleased.

Mark it well, God's love far surpasses the love of fathers. He won't despise a staple, or a widow's mite. He loves orange wrappers and dirty string.

We tend to look on the outward appearance, but God looks at the heart. He knows what we meant to say, what we intended to do, what we hoped to give.

Go ahead. Wrap you're heart in an orange wrapper and give it to Him. It'll make His day!

"Mommie, when is Sunday?" "Just two more days, Jane. Today is Friday."

"...And then will it be Sunday? And am I going to Sunday School?"

It wasn't so much the desire for Sunday School as it was [the opportunity to wear] those brand-new shiny slippers . . .

Sunday Slippers

those Sunday slippers.

Of course there never was a grown-up who looked forward to Easter with one eye on that delectable hat on the closet shelf or the new suit on the hanger, was there?

And how shall I greet Easter? With all the joyousness of a heart aglow with love for the risen Savior, with a solemn awareness of all it meant to Him . . . and with high anticipation of that day when we shall see Him face to face, our risen, victorious, Lord!

A t Aldrich Acres, "new" Easter clothes generally meant a reshuffling of closets and their contents. Not new—reassigned! Generally by Easter I'd grown into some of Jon's clothes. Becky inherited an outfit or two from her older sister, Jane. And so it went. It was not unusual for someone to drop off a "missionary barrel" of used clothes. Some acceptable, some pretty well used up. Needless to say, Mom always tried to have something "new" for each of us kids.

She knew from personal experience what it was like not to have adequate clothing. Here is what a friend recalled about their days working at a Christian conference center:

Throughout the summer conference Doris wore a green voile dress, morning to night, every day. It was the only dress she owned. She was exquisitely groomed and the dress was becoming. For variety she changed accessories. Neither of the girls mentioned it until after the conference, when Doris confided to Ruth that it had been a real trial to her. She, like any girl, liked pretty clothes and she could wear them with style.

Hudson Taylor once said, "We can afford to have as little as the Lord supplies." Think about it! Sometimes, in the best interest of the soul, less is better.

Yes, God understands the power of "Sunday Slippers." After all, He's got a father's heart.

A Thought for Others

How many times in the middle of a batch of muffins one is interrupted with, "Mommie, I want a digging spoon . . . I want a drink . . . I want a cracker. Mommie . . . I want my leggings off. . . ."

There are times when the mother just sits there at the mixing-board and wonders if the day will ever come when life will hold more than a series of "wants."

They are only children, the oldest nearing five, and, as such, are behaving in a perfectly normal fashion. The day will come when they will be less demanding and . . . will be able to sense the family as a unit having its desires and standards. We trust that the day will come when they, as mature men and women, will put the Lord's interests first, others second, and their own last . . .

We supply the "wants" of the moment, hustle the little interruptions out-of-doors, give the bottle to the eager little mouth, and then finish the muffins for lunch. As we measure the batter into the tins the question comes with sudden urgency. *"And where |am I| in relation to the Lord? Still at the "want" stage? Blind to the needs of others? Oblivious to the great desires of His heart for |me|, and for the world?"*

MY CHILDREN

They're funny little grubby things
That take your time each day,
They fight and grab and kick and scratch
While busy with their play.

They ruin rugs with stains
     and spots,
They mar the decorations,
Your precious books, your works
     of art——
Subject to desecrations.

They mean you have to do without
Your new Spring suit, or Fall——
It goes to buy their underwear
Their shirts and overalls.

You do not own a stylish car,
Canary birds that sing,
You do not have fine silverware,
You don't have *anything*.

Except the satisfaction
Which small children prove to be,
And strange as it may seem to some
Means more than all to me.

DORIS ALDRICH

No Love More Welcome Than His

"Mommie, how many times does Jesus love me?" asked five-year-old Jane who was busy with her bath one night. She paused, toothbrush in hand, and awaited the answer.

Mommie was drying lanky Jon, and while she rubbed away on a bony knee, answered, "Well, Janie, He loves you more than anyone else in the whole world." "But how many times?" persisted Jon as he thrust out a foot for the towel to dry. . . .

How many times does the Lord love me? What are the mathematics of heaven? "I have loved you with an everlasting love. From before the beginning until forever, He loves us. . . ."

"Mommie, when I get to heaven, I'm going to find the Lord Jesus and put my arms around Him and love Him. I know where the Lord Jesus will be in heaven. Right by the door, where everybody can find Him."

Yes, little girlie, He is right by the door and never was love more eager, nor welcome greater than His.

ow many times does God love you and me? I couldn't begin
to count the ways.

In eternity past, the Holy Trinity agreed upon the
creation of mankind even though it meant the Fall and the
Cross. Jesus agreed to become the Lamb of God who would
bare the punishment for sins that we deserved. Isn't that
love? "Greater love has no man than this, that a man lay
down his life for his friend."

Friends stick with you. They're loyal and trustworthy.
They enjoy you and you enjoy them; you laugh together
and sometimes share tears together. They rejoice when
you rejoice; they weep when you weep.

Jesus is the best friend to have. He knows everything
about you and says "I love you still." He accepts you
unconditionally, in spite of your failures.

Yes, little girlie, He is right by the door and He is
knocking. Don't leave Him standing outside—throw open
the door and invite Him in.

W hy do you whisper, Mommie?" asked Jon when prayer was finished.

"Because Joe is asleep," answered Mother, nodding her head toward Joe who was sprawled out in his crib across the room.

Love Hears the Slightest Whisper

"Can the Lord hear you when you whisper?"

"Yes, Jon, He can hear." (Oh blessed, blessed fact!)

"Why can He hear us?"

"Because He is God . . . and because He loves us . . ."

Can the Lord hear us when we whisper? What a blessedness to know that He can, and He does. The fact of His omnipresence and His love guarantees that He hears. Love does not have to be shouted at . . . love is always on the alert to hear even the slightest whisper.

How the heart can rest in the sufficiency of our God! When we are too tired to pray, when there is not time . . . when the pressure is great and the burdens pile up—just a whisper—and He is there. "Lo, I am with you always."

I n times of loneliness and in times of frantic business our faithful God is there. Back in the early 1930's Mother longed for marriage, home, and family. Her desire to be a partner in raising a Christian family seemed to dim with the passing of each year. Her longing for a husband and home sometimes overwhelmed her.

> One day when Ruth (a close friend) walked into her bedroom she heard someone sobbing in the clothes closet next to her room. She knocked on the door—no answer. She quietly opened the door and there sat Doris with one oxford on and the other one in her hand. She was plucking at the laces trying to undo them but was blinded by tears. "I want to be having a baby in the spring like Tony, Lois, and Evelyn," she cried (from Musing of a Mother, 61-62).

In spite of her loneliness, her desire to belong, to be part of a family, God continued to be her confidant. And in His perfect time He fulfilled her desires exceedingly, abundantly above what she could ask or think. Praise God, all nine of her children are serving Him today!

Jane was having her turn to "go with Daddy." She had enjoyed her visit to the printers and was quite at home among the office force at the Bible school, and now was having the thrill of sitting up to a lunch counter with him.

"Shall we say 'thank you' to God," her daddy asked? Bowing his head he mumbled a brief word of thanks and, like

Artless Simplicity

many, did it in such a manner that the waitresses or customers might think he was inspecting his soup, resting his eyes, or reading something near his plate.

When daddy's head arose, his five-year-old daughter was still sitting there with her dainty hands folded reverently under her bowed head—just as if she were at home where the giving of thanks is the accepted thing.

There are no doubt a number of reasons why the Lord Jesus Christ wanted the little children to come unto Him, but their artless simplicity and willingness to witness for Him must have a large place in His heart.

Kids have a way of slicing through the baloney and getting down to the basics, don't they? Our Lord, a lover of kids, told us that unless adults become like children and exercise child-like faith, they don't have a chance of seeing even the lights of the Kingdom of Heaven.

Kids need "laptime," and so do big people. Most people use "God," "Jesus," "Father" or "Lord" when they pray. Some struggle to call God "Father." Some visualize Him as a harsh, judgmental father. To others, "Lord" suggests austere power and sovereignty.

What if we called Him "Papa"? Through the Holy Spirit we cry "Abba" Father, and *abba* is the Aramaic word for "papa" or "daddy." We can enjoy the privilege of having "lap time" with a heavenly Abba who enjoys our fellowship.

So, go ahead, push open the doors to the heavenly throne room and head boldly for His lap. He'll squeeze you real good and be delighted you came.

Love Through Me

There in the center of the table lay Auntie Bessie's birthday box and around the table, a fringe of eager children. Becky, her blue eyes and button nose just table high—Jon, the lanky one. . . . Joe was fit to burst with importance. His boyish haircut made him look older than three and more than ever like his father. It was his day, his box, and his dark eyes shone with excitement. The cover is off and there are the gifts! "For Janie . . . for Jon . . . for Joe . . . and Joe." One tag reads, "For Joe to pass around," and Janie sidles up in sweet helpfulness (it might be candy). "I'll help you Joe," she purrs.

Her solicitous regard for Joe's well-being continued on into the next day. She moved her chair at the table in order to sit next to him. She lavished cream and sugar on his breakfast cereal and saw to it that he was well-provided with toast and jam. This gracious care lasted as long as Joe's candy.

Childlike and laughable, yes . . . but wait, are we ever the least bit guilty of discriminating among the Lord's own family? Do some seem to have the "candy" and others not? . . .

(con't.)

Should we not pray that the love of God be shed abroad in our hearts in such measure that the hungry, needy ones will be refreshed by a very real sense of love? *"Love them, Lord, through me. Not just all the loveable ones, but the needy ones who aren't so lovable, that these, too, may feel Thy love through me, and feeling it, may come to love Thee better."*

A THOUGHT FROM JOE

I saw a bumper sticker recently that asked the question *"If I followed you home, would you keep me?"* It's a poignant request, a painful question. Yet it touches all of us. Don't we all fear rejection when our candy runs out? We need someone to love and care for us . . . regardless.

Who will be there when our lives crumble like Humpty Dumpty. Who will be there to "put us together again"? Only our heavenly Father can do that. Even when all we have to offer Him are the broken pieces of our lives, He takes them and makes them into something beautiful and good.

A Gift Freely Given

J on appeared in the doorway and thrust a boyish fist at Mommie. It unfolded to reveal two pennies, a tax token, and a nickel. . . ."I want to earn this money," he said.

"But, Jon, Daddy gave it to you. Why do you want to earn it?"

"Oh, I just want to. I want to earn it," he answered rather vaguely.

"Well, Son, you see Daddy gave it to you for a gift because he wanted you to have it, so you can't very well *earn* that money. It is already yours. It has been given to you."

Funny how a little thing like that will get you started thinking. . . . There are so many grown folks who have the same trouble with God's gift of salvation. They want to earn it when all the time it is a gift! "For by grace are ye saved through faith, and that not of yourselves; it is the gift of God; Not of works lest any man should boast" (Ephesians 2:8-9). . . .

[Salvation is] a gift from God Himself. Take it . . . from His loving hand, knowing that you could never earn it—that you never *need* to earn it.

What goes through the mind of a four-year-old that makes him want to earn something he already possesses? The same thing that went through the mind of Martin Luther as he climbed the steps of the Basilica on his knees. In the midst of his penance the Spirit whispered, "the just shall live by faith."

Religion is spelled DO. Christianity is spelled DONE.

God stretches His hands out to us and invites us to receive, at no cost, the gift of new birth— salvation through His Son, Jesus Christ.

We want to make it complex, when it's really very simple. Christ has already done all the work. Now He offers us the gift. It doesn't have to be paid for. It must simply be accepted.

And that settles it.

Here Daddy comin'." shouts Joe from his lookout at the dining-room window. Before the car has slid into the garage, the four older children are at the kitchen door.

Mother calls to deaf ears, "Jane, Jon, Joe! It's too cold out without wraps. Wait until Daddy gets to the porch!" . . .

In they come, Daddy laden down with a bulging carton

Father-Love

of groceries and festooned with children. One swings on each leg and one grabs a coattail. . . .

What is that satisfying sense of treatment that settles over the household? Mommie's heart is warmed by it as she finishes up dinner. Why, it's just that Daddy's home.

And heaven will be satisfying because we are at home with our Father.

➤ Daddy was asleep on the couch. The twins, then only a few weeks old, were alongside him. Mommie picked up Timmie, the outside one, and Virginia suddenly missed him. She gave a sharp cry. Instantly Daddy's arm gathered her close and he roused up.

Our Heavenly Father is ever alert to the faintest cry of His weakest babe. And He "slumbers not nor sleeps," but His watch-care over us is constant and unfailing.

➤ Time to prune the cherry tree at the lower end of the orchard. (Those cherry pies all winter are worth it.) Daddy sallies forth, pruning equipment in hand. The four eldest also sally forth, trailing him in duck fashion. Jane, Jon, and Joe in "triplet" playsuits and Becky in bright blue leggings, scarlet sweater, and hood. It's a gala afternoon to have Daddy home, and the children's delight is endless. They scramble up and down the ladder, snatch the falling branches, and ask endless questions.

Companionship in the family has its counterpart in the relationship between our Heavenly Father and His children. "I and the Father are one," Jesus said (John 10:30).

➤ It is evening and almost bedtime. The living-room seems full to overflowing with pajama-clad youngsters. They scurry around, enjoying that bit of freedom before time to go upstairs. Daddy responds to their plea, "Let's play horse," and they all pile on while he crawls around the room. Becky, who gets the last chance on, usually falls off. The horse finally collapses under a load of four [squealing] horsemen and the game is over.

Daddy kneels at the living-room couch with Jane, Jon, and Joe alongside. Becky inspects the thrust-out feet of first one, then another. Then she runs to kneel beside Daddy, bunting and thrusting her way in until she is under his arm. *"And thank Thee for our home . . an' Mommie . . . an' Daddy . . . an' the two twins . . . 'an the cow. Amen. Now you pray, Joe,"* Jane adds.

Mommie, and Daddy, and home—a satisfying fellowship. "And truly our fellowship is with the Father and with His Son, Jesus Christ" (1 John 1:3).

"COMPENSATION"

Diapers by the dozen
Dishes by the score
"Formula" to struggle with—
And wait, there's even more . . .

Dust upon the table
Clothes upon the rack.
Beds which wait for making—
Of work there is no lack.

Baby's pink and twinkly toes,
Her little shouts of glee,
That sweet and charming
           sudden smile,
A dampish kiss for me.

At eventide a dear man's love,
Candlelight that glows,
A sense of deep abiding
           peace,
Of joy that overflows.

DORIS ALDRICH

THIS WAS MOTHER'S "FAMILY RECIPE."

1 Dear Husband   Faith, Hope, and Love
1 Cow
4 Girls   1 Sheep Dog
1 Eight Acre Place
4 Boys   1 Sweet Baby Girl
1 Fish Pond

Separate boys and girls. Mix well together, husband, horses, and cows.

Separate boys and fish pond. Put baby girl and sheep dog together patting gently. If mixture curdles, add husband to boys and "beat well." Allow time for ingredients to become well blended. Stir in ample quantities of faith, hope, and love being sure that these are evenly distributed.

Spread over an eight-acre place and garnish with twinkling stars and silver shafts of moonlight. If stars and moonlight are not at hand, try splashes of sunlight and a whistling wind.

He stood there, just inside the door. His hands were busy with a small bouquet of flowers and his work cap. The nurses hurried past him and so he stood, uncertain.

Mommie watched him from her hospital bed across the hall. Finally someone told him where he'd find "her," and with

A Quiet
that bit of a shy light in his face, he started [down the hall].

Gentleness
Just another father among many, many who have come through that doorway at the head of the stairs, and yet to him there was never such a baby and to them never such joy and fulfillment.

Mommie thought of how it was two weeks ago when Annette as born. After the long, hard time there was the awakening to a blessed quiet and to Daddy standing there. "And did you say it was a girl? . . . and is she all right? . . . did you say it was all over? . . . and is the baby all right?"

"Yes," Daddy replied. "And she looks just like me!" And she does.

There are three mothers who did not want their babies. There is one mother whose crying echoed down the corridor.

She lost her baby and she was inconsolable. (Oh, the push and pull of life one sees from a hospital bed!)

The nurses and the doctors tried to comfort the heart-broken mother but they could not. Sedatives brought only temporary quietness, . . . there was always the awakening to the loss. And then they moved her to another room, a room in which there was someone who could comfort her, a mother who had lost her baby, too.

Mommie could hear them talking, for their room was next to hers. In a few days there was even laughter, as the heartache eased a bit.

What a picture of a thing hard to express—the understanding gentleness of the Lord! The doctors, the nurses, the mothers who had their babies could not know the feel of empty arms and the aching loss. But the mother who had also lost her baby . . . she knew.

And when we come to the Lord with our burdens, our heartaches that no one knows—He understands. He can comfort, because He is "touched with the feelings of our infirmities," being "in all points tempted like as we are" (Heb. 4:15).

With the birth of Annette in 1944 mother had seven children under six years of age. Why so many children? Was she a naive country girl who didn't know any better?

Mother graduated from Biola College and the University of Washington and then went on to seminary in New York. She was a gifted, talented young woman who had an intense desire to serve the Lord. Raising a godly family was at the heart of her life's mission.

This is how Mother described the spiritual purpose she and Dad had for their family:

> "We are taking the long view and are seeing not just the lines of diapers and yowling babies, but we see our children grown and used of the Lord. We have the faith to expect them to be one of the outstanding Christian families."

I t was Monday. Mommie and the day looked at one another, and the day was bigger than Mommie.

There was twice the usual amount of daily washing (and seven kids to keep us well supplied). There was a messy house to straighten up, and there were six babies to care for on a rainy day.

God's Strength

After Daddy left with Jane for school, Mommie just sat and waited, and the children swirled and swarmed through the house.

When the Lord said, "My grace is sufficient for thee, for my strength is made perfect in weakness," did He really mean it? And is it not true that if we do not come to know the Lord in the circumstances of everyday life, we'll not come to know Him well?

Mommie thought . . . and the word came, "Come unto me all ye that labor and are heaven-laden and I will give you rest" (Matt. 11:28).

The day grew smaller when Mommie remembered, "I can do all things through Christ who strengthens me" . . . all things—even a houseful of children, a rainy day, and a Monday.

M y grace is sufficient for thee."

Grace can be translated "enablement," and *sufficient* means adequate. God's enablement is adequate even when children swirl and swarm through the house.

"*For my strength is made perfect in weakness.*" God's grace flows to our areas of weakness and vulnerability. His grace flows to those who acknowledge that their need is not partial, but total and complete.

Our responsibility as the "heavy-laden" is to come to God, and He promises to give us rest, to set our minds at ease, to restore our souls.

God's enablement is adequate, but not automatic. He invites us to bring our list of burdens to Him. Tell Him which ones you must deal with today and then wait for His enablement to meet your need.

When the day looms too large, let God be your strength. You *can* do all things through Him.

A Love Offering to the Lord

It was the biggest piece of money he had ever had, a whole half dollar. . . . Jon jingled it in his pocket along with the usual nails, pennies, pocketknife, and string. The rattle sounded much like Daddy's pocket, and he was pleased.

It was Sunday morning. Jon counted over his money. "I'll put the pennies and the butter token in Sunday school," he mused and went slowly on with his dressing.

"Why don't you put the big money into Sunday school, Jon?" asked Mommie. "It would make the Lord happy."

"Why don't *you* give me a big money to put in?" he countered. "I'll put the pennies in now and the next time I get a half dollar I'll put that in." he added. Thus satisfied, he jingled his full pocket and went down to breakfast.

A few days later when Mommie and Jon were shopping, they passed a candy counter. "Would my big money buy a box of that?" queried five-year-old Jon. Satisfied that it would, he eagerly handed the salesgirl his fifty-cent piece.

They walked down the street together, Mom and Jon. Every so often he reassured himself with, "I'm so glad I have that candy. I haven't got the money, but I have my candy."

Soon both candy and money were gone, and Jon was beginning to know something of investment, too young, perhaps to realize that he had missed a chance to invest for eternity.

But those of us who are older—do we sometimes make the same mistake? Things of earth seem so sweet and things of eternity so unreal and "for some other day when I get another big money."

Thanksgiving time is a wonderful opportunity to express the thankfulness of our hearts by a real love offering to the Lord. Because of all He is to us, because of all He did for us, our hearts should sing for joy and our gifts to Him should be lavish.

I t always seemed that by the third week of the month, our family funds were gone. In the early years, it was not unusual for Dad to receive no salary for several months at a time. So we picked strawberries, blackberries, and gooseberries. We sold apples, berries, and milk. We piped water to the neighbor who bought it from us. For years we dried boxes of prunes and canned hundreds of cans of fruit.

We stored squash and apples in a cool shed, checking them regularly for rot. We churned our own butter, made cottage cheese, baked our own bread, and raised our own beef, chickens, ducks, and turkeys. Our clothes? They were usually from the church "missionary barrel"—mostly hand-me-downs.

But don't think for one moment we felt deprived or disadvantaged. Even when Dad was traveling, we would have Sunday school at home and we always took an offering. We had no money, so we used buttons instead. It turns out the buttons worked just fine—we all learned to tithe, and God always provided for our every need.

He Wants the Love in Our Hearts

Mommie and the children were decorating the house for Christmas. The children were full of joyous excitement, and the house was full of bits of evergreen, pieces of tinsel, and broken silver balls. . . .

The children were nearly finished with their work and their faces were happy and satisfied. What [did it] matter that one branch of the tree was fairly drenched with silver rain and another had missed the shower altogether? (Mommie could readjust the rain later.)

"Mommie," asked Jane, "what makes everyone so happy at Christmas?"

"Well, because it is the Lord Jesus' birthday . . . and because we love Him . . . and because we are happy about His coming to this world."

Jane thought a minute and then said, "And is the Lord happy about you?"

Oh, little girlie, what a question you've asked. Is the Lord happy about us on His birthday? Really happy because He

(Con't)

sees within our hearts a deep, true love for Him? A satisfying love and not just a seasonal affection, stirred up by the festivities of Christmas?

Does He see our Christmas activities centered in a love for Him or is the festivity itself the center? It makes a difference, because what He wants more than anything else on His birthday is the love in our hearts.

A THOUGHT FROM JOE

God is the happiest, most joy-filled being in the universe. And why shouldn't He be? He has you as His child, and He's tickled about you.

He likes your spunk. The twinkle in your eyes brings Him great delight. Even your moments of rebellion don't greatly concern Him. He disciplines you when it's appropriate, and nothing can thwart His purposes for your life. He knows that a day is coming when all His children will be fully mature sons and daughters.

Joy is a victory signal. It is the quiet confidence that what God has begun He will accomplish because He is in charge of the details of our lives.

Timmie-the-twin climbed up onto Mommie's lap, and Virginia scrambled up on Daddy's. Mommie pulled Becky's highchair close, and Jon moved his chair over to her. Jane edged up near to Daddy, and we were ready for our morning devotions at the breakfast table. But not quite ready for Joe was left alone at one side of the table.

A Separate Loneliness

"I want someone to be close to," remarked Joe in a wistful sort of way.

Daddy reached out his arm and pulled Joe's chair right up next to himself and cuddled his brown-eyed "replica" close.

"I want someone to be close to" . . . How it expresses the cry of every heart! It would seem that God has put within each one of us a separate loneliness that cries out to be satisfied. And satisfaction does not lie in things or in people. The lonely place is only filled and satisfied by God Himself.

Sometimes we fill our lives so full that the cry of the lonely place is not heeded. But it is there.

Perhaps this coming year will take away from us some of the things and some of the people we've substituted for God, and our need of Him will stand revealed. "I want someone to be close to". . . and He will be there—there with all His satisfying presence.

A THOUGHT FROM JOE

Three-Corner Rock is one of my lonely places. My fourth-grade teacher, Mr. Scott, spent summers manning forest service lookouts there. He told marvelous stories about plants and animals, hikes and waterfalls, secret pools, forest fires and campfires. We could smell the food, watch sparks fly into the night, hear the kindling crack and pop, and watch the fading glow of the last embers.

A dozen years later I spent a summer at Three-Corner Rock. There was no electricity, no running water, no telephones, no mail delivery, or maid service. The days were wonderful, but as eventide came and clouds of darkness crept up the valley floor, a wave of loneliness swept across me.

Sometimes I would sit on the railing as darkness came and sing out at the top of my voice. Other times I would cry out to God. Sometimes I'd play my trumpet, sending its music rebounding from peak to peak.

"God, it seems, has put within our hearts a separate loneliness that cries out to be satisfied." I agree with Mother and would suggest that He, too, longs for us to be close to Him.

It was one of those mornings. Daddy was downstairs getting breakfast. Mommie was up in the large bathroom dressing babies.

Becky was as full of wiggles. . . . Jane, the oldest, seemed unmoved by the repeated warning that if she didn't hurry she

Kindness In the Family

would be late to school. (First graders apparently don't care!) Jon and Joe fought over which one should have the fluffy peach bathmat to dress on. (Neither wanted the old green one.) The

small twins wandered soggily from washbowl to bathtub nibbling soap at both places in spite of emphatic "no, no's" from Mommie. . . .

Jane's braids were harder to do than usual, and she was very cross. The children seemed unmoved by Mommie's efforts to hurry them, and the fussing continued. She finally said, "You know, there's a verse in the Bible which says, 'Be ye kind one to another'" (Eph. 4:32).

"Well, there's no strangers here," remarked Jane. "There's only the family." And Mommie laughed right out loud much to everyone's open-mouthed amazement. So often it IS that way. The lovely Christian graces seem easier to manifest outside the home. And yet no one needs them more than the ones who have to live with us!

J ump-starting a passel of sleepy, kids is not an easy task.
With no heat in the upstairs we were not excited about
having to bail out onto a cold floor. Some of the events of
getting dressed were very territorial. Jane claimed both the
best bathmat and the location closest to the sink. Most
mornings one or two of the kids wandered aimlessly, a
tooth-brush dangling from their lips. A tug-of-war over a
towel or a bar of soap was a daily occurrence.

Some would plop down on the bath mat and go back to
sleep. Others wandered down the hall like little lost sheep
who had gone astray. What does it take to shepherd your
flock? A sense of humor is a must! A parcel of patience will
go a long way, and faith in your joint-venture-Father who
resides in heaven is a must.

Lord, how can you be glorified in this early morning
mess? We know you understand the swift pace of life and
delight to enroll us in Family 103—a class that begins the
moment baby makes an appearance. Fortunately, raising kids
is a joint-venture process between parents and God. And we
can rest in the knowledge that He understands and gives us
wisdom and strength—and a good laugh once in a while to
keep us going.

Timmie, the twin, would not eat his dinner. . . .
Mommie tried to cajole him by "take a bite for Daddy,
for Jon, for Jane." He would take a bite for no one, and
that was that. Daddy took a hand in it. "I'll take him up by me"
he said. . . . "Now, Timmie, you take up that spoon and eat."

Fellowship with the Father

Timmie only
slumped the further
and glowered the harder. He
eyed Daddy from lowered
brow, exhibiting a Churchillian
expression. Daddy looked at
Mommie with an I-hope-this-comes-out-all-right look, and
announced, "Timmie, if you don't pick up that spoon and eat
I'm going to spank you hard."

Timmie stared at his food and thrust out his lip. He
would not look at Daddy. And so he was paddled warmly
and put back into his chair. Whereupon he picked up his
spoon and ate and more—he smiled.

After dinner, when Daddy was settled with the evening
newspaper, Timmie came and bunted his way up under the
paper and onto Daddy's lap. He flopped his curly blond head

down on Daddy and he looked at him and grinned. His light
hair on Daddy's red sweater and his big smile were charming.
In contentment he rocked back and forth.

What made the difference?

NOW his heart was obedient and he was in fellowship
with his father and there was "nothing between."

And so it is with those who know the Lord. If we would
have that nearness, that resting in the Lord, then there must
be obedience and unbroken fellowship. . . .

Do we feel as near to the Father's heart as Timmie did
to his Daddy's? Do we feel free to be that close? He wants us
to, and He has made full provision for our restoration to
fellowship when our disobedience raises a barrier between
us. "If we confess our sins, he is faithful and just to forgive
us our sins, and to cleanse us from all unrighteousness"
(1 John 1:9).

Daddy enjoyed the nearness even more than Timmie,
and he rested his chin on that blonde curly head with heart
satisfaction. Are we bringing to our heavenly Father's heart
a joy and satisfaction because we are close to Him?

A THOUGHT FROM JOE

L ord, I see the trapeze You're sending my way. I know it will be of great benefit to let go of mine and catch Yours. My knuckles are white. I must let go to latch on. I must give up to catch up. Give me the grace to grasp the centrality of Your promises, the wonder of Your person. Enable me, oh God to let go of distorted images of who You are and what You do. Let me find pleasure in calling out, "Father, Father."

May the wind carry my call to Your throne.

The stars were as bright as Becky's eyes and as shiny as her little round face. It was going to frost tonight so Mommie was out hanging clothes. (It whitens them to be all "frosting in the morning," as the children say.)

Down over the hill the lights in the houses shone out

Upheld by God's Power

into the darkness. The frogs were beginning to sing in the pond in the back pasture. Spring was a-promised in spite of the frost.

Mommie looked at the stars while she hung the washing on the line. She thought of the faithfulness of God who placed them and kept them there. Faithful to the stars and faithful to mothers, too.

There was last month when six of the Aldrich had hard chickenpox at once. The days (and nights!) were so full that mother felt driven. Becky wailed, "These sheegun-pogs they scratch-a my tummy."

When the burden was almost too heavy and the heart cried out, there was the Lord and His sufficiency and one could rest. "Fear thou not; for I am with thee: be not dismayed; for I am thy God. I will strengthen thee; yea, I will help thee: yea I will uphold with the right hand of my righteousness" (Isa. 41:10). . . .

Thank God for the experiences of going through . . . with Him!

(Con't)

The clear frosty air made Mommie's fingers tingle and she hurried a bit faster. . . . The wind blew a bit until the clothes stirred and the stars shone far away and bright. One last look at them before going in . . . one long look and then a prayer of thankfulness for the God "who upholdeth all things by the word of His power"—even Mothers with a houseful of sick babies.

A THOUGHT FROM JOE

Lift your eyes to the heavens. Who made all these? He who brings forth the starry hosts one by one and calls them each by name and not one of them is missing (Isa. 40:26).

What a startling, profound truth. The Shepherd of the stars leads them out, calls them by name, and always knows where they are—they are never lost. Should we not trust the One who packed one-million galaxies in the bowl of the Big Dipper and knows the names of all the stars in all of the galaxies? Does He not care diligently for each of us?

Plant firmly in your mind that the God who knows and positions the stars knows who you are, where you are, what you need, and where you are going. Mix these great truths about God into the problems you face, blend them until the lumps are gone, add a few tears, sprinkle with biblical promises, and reaffirm your faith in the Shepherd of the stars.

Baby Annette was having her bath. The usual audience of brothers and sisters leaned over the edge of the tub. They commented on her splashing hands, her dark hair and the way it curled in the back when it got wet. "Isn't she sweet, Mommie? Aren't we glad she is our baby?"

They continued to toss in things for "Net-Net" to play with

Smiling

Hearts

—blocks, soap, boats and fish, until the baby was surrounded with toys that bobbed on the water just out of reach. . . .

Joe looked at her and said, "Mommie, is everyone born to smile?"

And what could Mommie say? . . . One doesn't look at a brown-eyed, four-year-old, all sweet with childlike eagerness, and answer "no." She satisfied him with a happy reply, and he went on about his own play. . . .

"*Is everybody born to smile?*" Would that it were true! But Mommie . . . knew that it was not so. Life is not all smiles for everyone. For many it is often less of smiles and more of tears.

Not born into this world to smile—that's true. But there is one "world" into which we're born to smile—even in the midst of sorrow. And that is when we accept the Lord Jesus Christ as our Savior and are born again into new life and hope in Christ. Then, because we are His and know Him, we can smile no

(Con't)

matter how hard the way or how great the burden—because He is there.

It will not be just our lips smiling but our "hearts" smiling, too, because it comes from an inexhaustible supply of the joy of the Lord and the peace of God.

A THOUGHT FROM JOE

Sometimes we smile inwardly as we observe or remember something from our past. There are memories that tickle us, that make us chuckle each time they are resurrected—and that's good for the soul.

President Lincoln said that after forty an individual is responsible for his own face. He wasn't talking about cosmetics that come in a case or a can. He was talking about the cosmetics of the soul.

By age forty the face reveals the condition of the heart. If the heart is hard, the face broadcasts it. There's no sparkle, no twinkle, no vitality, no joy. If the heart is tender towards the Lord, however, you can't help but see the joy spread all over the face.

Turn your eyes upon Jesus . . . He can make something beautiful—not just out of your face but out of your life as well!

I t wasn't a very large meeting but what it lacked in size it made up in enthusiasm. Becky perched on the kitchen stool; Timmie and Virginia, the twins, sat in high chairs. Jane, Jon and Joe lined up the old dining room chairs and sat on them. The neighbor children used a table leaf placed between the twins' small white chairs.

The Song of Faith

It was Sunday afternoon; we were having a Sunday school. Daddy was the teacher, Mommie the pianist, and Jane took up the offering (of buttons!).

We sang awhile and then Daddy talked. We sang again followed by a time of prayer. Jon thanked the Lord for quite a list while Mommie tried to make the twins stay down in their high chairs.

Then it was time to sing again, and once more Mommie was sorely tried because one piano key refused to sound. . . .

Mommie thought of how that one key was just like a lot of Christians. If only ONE is silent and fails to contribute, how much of melody and harmony is lost in the great song of Christian faith!

And then, if someone is counting on us and we don't respond—it's a loss, and a disappointment.

Just a repair needed and a bit of tuning to get back into the song—and how worthwhile to be there!

here were no robes, there were no stained glass windows (that's not to say there were no *stained* windows) or padded pews. The furniture was an eclectic collection of distressed pieces some would call Early Salvation Army.

Sometime before the service began, mother would be sure each of us, including visitors, had a button or two for the offering.

What did the Heavenly Father think about buttons and stuck keys and wiggly children? He loved it. In fact, I suspect He shut down the heavenly worship service, quieted the choirs, hushed the angels, pointed towards earth and proclaimed, "Look at those kids, bless their hearts. Now *they* know how to worship!"

The hosts of heaven probably laughed about the silent piano note and the button offering. As the children prayed, God dispatched flocks of angels to answer those prayers. And while there wasn't much to be done about Dad's monotone voice, no one could deny the faith that stood behind it.

The family of God will build itself up in love in response to the proper working of each individual part—and home is where it starts.

This Will Be Heaven

The children were finishing their lunch. Timmie and Virginia, the twins, were over by the dining-room window eating at their own small table. Every so often the white ruffled curtains suffered a tug from sticky, little fingers. Jon studied a bread crust and with a dreamy expression asked, "What will we do the first thing in heaven, Mommie?" Mommie paused in buttering bread and answered, "What would you like to do, son?" The others all hastened to speak and the twins looked up, surprised at the sudden outburst of conversation.

"I would like to thank the Lord for all the things and because He loves us," said Jon. Joe hastened to add, "I'd like to start playing. Will there be toys and things?"

Jane looked up from her dish of carrots. "Well, I'd like to go for a walk with the Lord Jesus and all the angels." Mommie smiled to herself as she thought how *many* there would be. . . .

"What do you want to do first, Mommie?" they asked. *What do I want to do first?* How can one tell them what it will mean to see Him, to look into His face, to feel that nearness of His dear presence? How can one express what it will mean to know heart-yearning fully satisfied?

(Con't)

Only the measure of longing here gives an indication of what it will be to see Him there, "whom having not seen, we love." And to be in His presence unashamed, complete in Him—all because of what He did for us! This will be heaven.

And so Mommie looked at them and answered. "The first thing I want to see is the Lord Jesus." And they were satisfied.

A THOUGHT FROM JOE

The reality of heaven should compel us to live differently. Our earthly home should not be our focus.

"By faith [Abraham] dwelt in the land of promise as in a foreign country . . . for he waited for the city which has foundations, whose builder and maker is God" (Heb. 11:9–10).

"[Moses chose] rather to suffer affliction with the people of God rather than enjoy the passing pleasures of sin . . . for he looked to the reward" (Heb. 11:25–26).

Abraham and Moses made very difficult choices based on their understanding of the real estate of heaven and their future hope.

This world is not our home, we're just passing through on our way to that celestial city we will someday inherit as home. *"In my Father's house are many mansions."*

A new year, a new day, a new chance, a new person—a new anything stirs one's heart. And why? Because we've all known failure, discouragement, and disappointment, and with wishful longing we desire to start afresh. . . .

January is the month of the stiff upper lip and freshly starched stamina. But what of February, June, and October

A New Opportunity

when one's resolutions are blunted and one's stamina worn thin? Is there not some way out? Some sufficiency?

The answer is God—His grace is sufficient to enable the weakest, and His power alone can keep.

Those of us who spend much time over the mixing bowl, who tread the daily round, who tuck small fuzzy-tops into bed at the end of a long, weary day—whose patience and grace give out—find a wonderful opportunity to prove for ourselves the truth of our Lord's word: "My grace is sufficient for thee, for my strength is made perfect in weakness."

A THOUGHT FROM JOE

J anuary should be a time not only for resolution, but
also for reflection. It's not a bad idea to temper our
resolutions with our reflections. We have feet of clay, we're
prone to wander, we don't trust, and we don't obey.
But genuine humility attracts the enablement of God: "My
grace is sufficient for thee, for my strength is made perfect in weakness."

They all went along to get "Piggus." Daddy had two children in the front seat and Mommie had five in back with her, and no one felt any loneliness of far distances! The trailer rolled along behind the car.

We ate crackers; we stopped for drinks of milk from the jar Mommie had brought along. We sang together, and we

The Joy of Togetherness

counted white horses and Black Angus cows. And when we got there we visited awhile, then loaded on the pig and started back home. . . .

We stopped for ice-cream cones, the first the twins had ever eaten. As we drove along Jon remarked, "It was nice of Uncle Gordon to give us that pig so we'll have some bacon."

"You shouldn't say 'Gordon,'" admonished Jane. "He isn't really our uncle. So you should say 'Uncle Fraser.' And they gave us some scrawberrie jam too."

They were tired and fussy as they neared home and very conscious of one another's feet and elbows. Finally, they were

home. While Daddy settled "Piggus" in the barn, Mommie fixed
a bottle for Annette and hurriedly prepared supper. Scrambled
eggs, freshly-made cottage cheese, bread, jam, tea, and the fat,
yellow pitcher of milk were soon ready. We ate in the kitchen
because it was so late, and the tired children were soon ready
to be tucked into bed.

Mommie thought of the trip and of how she enjoyed it.
The secret of it all was the sense of "togetherness"—the
thought of the whole family complete. And suddenly Mommie
realized that it would not always be so—someday they would
be separated and the thought hurt.

There is only one guarantee that any family will be
together forever even though separated by long distances.
(Nearness is a thing of the heart, and distance is not
concerned primarily with miles.)

The guarantee is the oneness that comes when each
member of the family knows and loves the Lord Jesus Christ
as Savior and the whole family is united in Him.

There can be nothing more important than to so live and
pray that our children will come to know the Lord.

Studies have shown that one of the most influential factors in the life of a child is what the father says at the dinner table. I believe that is true. Every morning, every evening, seven days a week the Aldrich family took time for devotions. They were short and sweet sometimes but were nevertheless a formative experience. In the evening we'd usually pray around the table. The older ones were each assigned a village in Thailand to pray for daily. And so we did. My village was among the Lisu people living in a remote mountain area. I prayed for them for years.

It was not unusual to discuss things of God for thirty to forty minutes after evening devotions. Of course, we had no television to rob us of this critical time of learning and being *together*. On one occasion Dad went to sleep while praying and mumbled something about God's blessings on the cows of the A-1 Dairy. Needless to say, we nearly died laughing. Those were fun times. (Incidently, the motto of the A-1 dairy was "You can whip our cream, but you can't beat our milk.")

Togetherness is all the family rushing to get the hay in the barn before the storm hits.

Togetherness is swimming at the Lewis River.

Togetherness is wrestling with Dad.

Togetherness is squeezing nine kids into our car—an old funeral hearse.

Togetherness is planning and participating in family worship services—complete with buttons for offerings.

Togetherness is the silence in a room while each one enjoys reading something of value, like the *Washington Farmer* or the *Reader's Digest*.

Togetherness is the whole family sleeping out on mattresses in the orchard.

Togetherness is functioning together when the electricity goes out for sixteen days.

Togetherness is standing together against that which is evil.

Togetherness is rallying together when someone is hurt or threatened.

Togetherness is each one doing his chores.

Togetherness is each one making the decision to follow God and then doing it.

In Christ, we can be together forever!

I t was the time of the alfalfa harvest and Daddy wanted to get the hay undercover before the rains came. With a sense of urgency, everyone pitched in and worked hard. For several days from early morning until late at night they focused on one objective—get the hay into the barn before the rain got it wet.

Mommie hustled the children to bed, and when they were

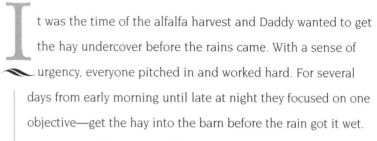

A Precious Harvest

asleep she went on up to the hayfield. The sun had just set and the glory of the evening was flung across the sky. The distant fir trees were sharply silhouetted against the glowing color. A clean, sweet wind whisked across the field and low in the south the puffy clouds piled in great heaps of gray. The bullfrogs in the swamp were tuning up for an evening of special music.

Babe (our horse) pulled the loaded hay-sled and obligingly stopped by each shock and waited patiently while it was loaded on . . . Mommie had a hayfork (and used it too), but it was so new to her that she was not a great help. But she enjoyed being there and she thought of this—

Is there any such willingness to work together and giving of one's strength in the Lord's harvest? . . . The millions of souls are precious to the Lord—but do we care? Care until it compels us to action?

I was four years old when this story was recorded. There isn't much a four-year-old can contribute to the serious task of gathering the hay. None of us children were capable of using a pitchfork with any degree of safety. We would grab armloads of hay and drag them to the sled, and one of us served as the official "stomper," packing the hay down into the sled.

Sometimes Dad would let us lead Babe to the next shock. Barely able to reach her bridle, we proudly towed her in the right direction. She was docile and fully cooperative. It was a heady experience.

The most fun, of course, was riding in the sled on the way to the barn. Dad would shout at us to "hold on," and then he'd get Babe running. Mother was a little nervous about it, but Dad assured her we'd be okay—and most of the time we were.

Friends and neighbors always pitched in to help with the harvest, and most of the time we beat the rain. When neighbors and friends are involved in such a common cause a special bonding takes place. The very word *neighbor* comes from a root that means "to draw near." And these are the ones we are called to love into the kingdom. Our mandate is to *love* them, not *evangelize* them. Paul made himself a servant "to win as many as possible." No serving, no winning.

Baby Annette was cuddly, soft, and sun-tanned.

Mommie was playing with her and enjoying her first attempts at walking. Her fat bare feet went spat-spat along the floor. Frequently she sat down hard. Mommie swooped her up and squeezed her until she squeaked . . .

Joe stood by watching. He said in a wistful sort of way, "I wish you loved me the way you do Net-Net."

"Why, Joe, I do. I love you all the time." Mommie held tight to Annette who

Loving Hands

was jumping in her arms.

"No you don't," he answered. "You don't love me with your hands."

Oh little hungry-hearted boy. . . . You are one with all of us in wanting warmth and nearness in your love.

How the Lord understood our hearts. He called the children unto Himself; He took them in His arms and blessed them. Their mothers would have been thankful for just the blessing, but the children never forgot the warmth and strength and tenderness of those dear arms. It made His love real to them.

And then there was the leper so full of loathesomeness. All men shrank from him until his heart was as sick as his body. One came, whose love saw past the dread disease to the greater need. He stretched forth His hand to him and brought healing to his body and a great surging warmth to his soul.

Oh, what a Savior! Touched with the feeling of our infirmities and knowing our need of love. . . . And didn't He "love us with His hands?" He drew us to Himself with them. . . . They were nail-pierced on the Cross for us.

Theological discussions were not unusual events at Aldrich Acres. The subject before us was God's love. The older children were affirming God's love for the whole world, but that was too impersonal for Becky, aged three. It was not enough to be just one among a great unnumbered group that He loved. "No," she insisted, "He does not love every bodies. He loves Becky."

My grandmother Ida May Aldrich, put it this way:

In Creation's early dawn
Did He love us—love us then?
Echoes back the matchless Word—
"My delights were with the sons of men."
Did He love us, love us still,
When man by transgression fell?
Speaks the Manger and the Cross,
Aye—He loved us, loved us well.
Tell me—did His love avail?
Did it save from death and hell?
Yes—the empty tomb reveals—
The living Way with Christ to dwell.
Aye—He loves us, loves us well.

His love touches all His children. The least we can do is "Reach out and touch someone"—today!

J ust two little boys dressed in their old overalls—they stood in front of the untrimmed Christmas tree, their eyes starry with anticipation and their minds turning over a dozen delightful dreams. Mommie was upstairs hanging the freshly ironed curtains. Christmas was coming. Everything must be ready for the loveliness of [Christ's] day. His birthday . . . how we all looked forward to it. The cleaning and decorating were done for His sake—that it might be beautiful for Him.

We Love Thee Lord

Joe and Jon looked at the tree, and though they were only four and five they knew it was for His birthday. . . .

They looked and looked, talking the while of Christmas. Finally Jon bowed his head and said, "Dear Lord, we love Thee. Amen." And Joe repeated—"Dear Lord, I love Thee. A-man."

And Mommy blinked back sudden tears. What a child's love must mean to Him! And how He must rejoice on His birthday at such a pure, sweet gift as this. What better gift for His day than loving hearts?

Jane said one time, "Mommie, when I go to heaven, I'm going to take the Lord a bag of candy." When told that wouldn't be quite possible, she answered, "Well, then I'll put a piece in my pocket for Him." And Mommie let it go at that because it was hard to explain to a little girl that we could not take a gift in our own hands to Him. . . .

Yes, the only gift we can give to Him on His day must be one of the intangibles—our love, our loyalty, our heart devotion.

It had been a long, full, rainy day and now at the close of it Mommie was tired. She sat down on Jane's bed to rest and talk. The pink walls, the blue drapes, the white ruffed curtains (which needed washing!) were a welcome change from the mussy kitchen and the untidy living room.

Sloshing Through the Mud

Downstairs there was the daily washing yet to be folded and put away—the house to straighten up and Jane's and Jon's school clothes to put in order for the morning. But for now it would be good to rest a minute up here and talk with her eldest. The other six were asleep.

Jane was full of questions (as are all seven-year-olds): "Why doesn't the Lord answer our prayers?" she asked, rather bluntly.

"Well, He does, dear," answered Mommie.

"No. He doesn't always. . . . The other day when that big wind blew so hard and Jon and I were walking home from school we were scared and asked the Lord to stop the wind and He didn't. We had to come home right through it."

"But you did get home, didn't you, dear? And safely. The Lord sometimes lets us go through hard things instead of taking them away. And He goes with us, and we come to know Him better because of the hard thing."

(Con't)

"Well . . . " answered Jane, still a bit mystified. She would

learn as she grew older to say:

"We thank thee, Lord, for pilgrim days

When desert streams were dry;

When first we learned what depth of need

Thy love could satisfy."

A THOUGHT FROM JOE

We all have those days, rare as they may be, when God seems to be focusing all His attention upon us as though He had invited us to a private photo shoot and spared no expense for film, flash bulbs, and special effects. Those who wait upon the Lord experience sacred moments when like eagles, they mount up and soar above the mountain peaks. There are times when those who wait experience enablement as they run and long-term stability as they walk.

It's sloshing through the mud and rain that teaches us the lessons about life's pain and struggles. We don't usually grow as much "mounting up with wings as eagles" as we do handling the daily wind and rain.

Footprints Along the Way

Jon was home from school with mumps. His cheeks were as round as any squirrel's at nut-gathering time. Jane had gone to school alone, and a second-grader is glad to have company on the walk home. Mommie waited until 3:30, and then she and Tipper [the sheep dog] started up the road. Tip bounded on ahead and made quick sallies into the alfalfa fields by the roadside. . . .

[Mommie] looked . . . and there was Jane, her eldest, running toward her with pigtails flying in the wind. Tipper, Mommie, and Jane were all mixed up for a few minutes of joyous confusion, and then they started home.

They walked down the gravel road, Jane on one smooth track and Mommie on the other. . . . They talked about the day at school . . . the lovely puffy clouds . . . the way that Cinnamon's smooth brown hide glistened in the sunshine as she grazed in the lower pasture.

Jane looked down at the muddy road and remarked, "Look, Mommie, I can see your footsteps all the way home." Sure enough, my footsteps were on Jane's side of the road, and she was walking home on the footprints Mommie made when coming to meet her at the bus stop.

Footprints all the way home, and footprints made in coming after me to take me home . . . someone walking alongside me on the way home.

There was One who came a long way from His home to meet us. But when He met us it was not to find us cheerily disposed toward Him. No, He sought us out, and He found us lost in sin. He took us to Himself and cleansed our hearts, delivered us from our misery, and freed us from our bondage.

How could He do this? Because the way He had come had led Him to the cross, there to settle the question of our sin by His death for us.

And now that we are walking along toward HOME, oh blessed thought, He walks alongside. Do we notice the footprints He made in coming after us? Are we constantly aware that the reason we are safely and surely going Home is because He came for us?

And the joy of His presence with us on the road Home . . . is it not deep and satisfying? It may be that we are so preoccupied that we've almost forgotten He is there. Do we talk about this and that with Him and experience the delight of His presence?

Or do we trudge glumly on our way hardly aware of the footprints or of that dear Person who is walking along with us?

L ooking back we see the footprints of Christ's coming.

Job said, "I know that my redeemer lives, and that He will stand at the latter day upon the earth." The footprints of Christ's coming began before the creation of the universe, when He agreed to make the journey and become the Redeemer of mankind.

Looking forward, we can see the footprints of His coming again. "If I go," He said, "I will come again and take you to Myself, that where I am, there you may be also" (John 14:3). He will come, not as the Lamb but as the Lion of the Tribe of Judah. What a glorious day of victory, of celebration, of joy!

In the meantime, He walks alongside us on our journey Home. He leads us each step of the way. He has gone before us . . . we can trust Him to lead us firmly, faithfully all the way.

I t was Jane's eighth birthday and Mommie wanted to make it a special day for her. One of the things Jane wanted was "a pair of white shoes to play nurse in.". . .

Aunt Bessie asked Mommie to look for the shoes for her to give to Jane. Mother looked and looked—they cost more than shoes-to-play-nurse-in should cost.

Never Too Busy

The upstairs shoe man said he didn't know where there would be any just like Mommie had in mind, and she was fairly discouraged. Portland was so big, the shoes so little . . . how could she find them?

She thanked the man at Lipman's and took the elevator down. It was sort of a weary day after all. Of course, Jane didn't have to have those shoes—and yet they would meet such a great desire. Mommie wanted them even more than Jane.

She started out the door to go over to Buster Brown's, and then *Someone* suggested, "Why not see what they have in the Downstairs Store?"—Someone who knew about little girls who loved Him . . . and big girls, too.

Mommie explained to the shoe man about nurse's uniforms and eight-year-olds. . . . He ducked in behind the racks and came out with white leather shoes, size 3 1/2, a plain slip-on, nurse-type shoe. Mommie's heart pounded. "How much are they?" she asked, wondering how he could hear the question above the singing joy within.

(Con't)

"A dollar ninety-nine . . . that's greatly reduced. They were upstairs."
He went away to wrap them up, and Mommie sat there blinking back the
tears. The piles of shoe boxes, the mirrors, and displays faded away. It
seemed as if just two were there, the dear Lord who had a thought for a
little girl, and Mommie. All she could say was "Oh dear Lord . . . oh dear,
dear Lord—thank Thee for Thy love."

A little thing for God to be bothering with you say? No—it is His same
great love that gave His Son to die that does the thoughtful and tender
things, too.

The man gave Mommie the package and she took it with rejoicing. The
sunshine of the day was no brighter than the light in her heart. God was
not too busy to think of a mother's love and a little girl's desire.

A THOUGHT FROM JOE

It's an awesome thing that God should desire to go shopping with His
children. To stash away just the right size shoe, perfect in every detail,
greatly reduced in price, . . . to shift the inventory so that the shoes were
in the right place, at the right time, at the right price . . . and doing it for
sheer pleasure. God answered Mother's prayer—give glory for that! It wasn't
a big deal from the Father's point of view. It *was* a big deal from Mother's.

God knew that those white miracle-shoes would be a significant
signpost on her pilgrimage of faith—another snapshot of the Father
caring for two of His daughters.

God our Father does the thoughtful and tender things.

It was sunset time. Mommie and Daddy and seven children walked up through the orchard to the upper pasture to see the loveliness flung out across the sky.

The field was large and the alfalfa deep, deep to the children anyway. They scattered and ran toward the sunset, enjoying the color and also the cool evening breeze.

He Holds
Our Hand

The three-year-old twins with their curly heads looked like two golden dandelions gone to seed. Jon and Joe ran in great sweeping circles. Tipper, the sheep dog, bounded after them.

Soon it was time to go back down to the house. The color faded, the tall fir trees stood out more black against the darkening sky. The children gathered close to Mother and Daddy. Mommie found herself walking back with little "Deedah" (Virginia) the twin alongside.

The field was large, the dusk was coming on. Home seemed quite far away to such a little one. "You hold my hand, Mommie. You hold my hand back to home." And Mommie held on tight.

(Con't)

As they walked along, Mommie thought of going Home . . . the gathering darkness, but One there holding our hand—"to home." And then we were there in the warmth and fellowship of home. Someday we'll be There—with Him. Home forevermore!

A THOUGHT FROM JOE

Do you know where your children are? If the growing darkness is settling upon them and their world, is your hand available to lead them home? Pray that God will extend the kingdom of light over the kingdom of darkness until "all the children are in." Give Him your hand. Give Him your children. Take comfort in knowing that where there is a pile of sin, there is a mountain of grace. Where there is failure, there is forgiveness; where there is despair, there is hope; where there is alienation, there is reconciliation.

ARE ALL THE CHILDREN IN?

I think ofttimes as the night draws nigh
Of an old house on the hill,
Of a yard all wide and blossom-starred
Where the children played at will.
And when the night at last came down,
Hushing the merry din,
Mother would look around and ask,
"Are all the children in?"

'Tis many and many a year since then,
And the old house on the hill
No longer echoes to childish feet,
And the yard is still so still.
But I see it all, as the shadows creep,
And though many the years have been
Since then, I can hear mother ask,
"Are all the children in?"

I wonder if when the shadows fall
On the last short, earthly day,
When we say good-bye to the world outside,
All tired with our childish play,
When we step out into that Other Land
Where mother so long has been,
Will we hear her ask, just as of old,
"Are all the children in?"

AUTHOR UNKNOW

Taste and See

Mommie was baking a cake and Net-Net was standing nearby to watch and to "lick." Because her chubby two-year self was not very tall, she ran to get one of the twins' chairs to stand upon. Now she was at the right licking height.

She eyed Mommie, wondering just when it would be safe to begin. Soon a little pink finger was thrust forth and right down into the mixing-bowl. Mommie said nothing, and her silence was encouragement. (They are "just past two" for so short a while.) The fingerful of cake batter was popped into an eager little mouth. Her dark brown eyes were full of enjoyment. The finger came back for more. . . .

Mommie thought of the verse, "O taste and see that the Lord is good: blessed is the man that trusteth in Him." The writer of that verse must have known the sweetness of the Lord and longed to have others know it, too.

A taste of a good thing creates a desire for more. Mommie thought of the Lord's tender, gracious love in all its many manifestations . . . the needs that were supplied almost before asking; the sense of His nearness in the hard places; the comfort for dark days; and the fellowship of joy in days of delight.

"The Lord is good . . . just taste and see."

Augustine, the great theologian, said, "Thou hast made us for Thyself, O God, and our hearts are restless until they find their rest in Thee." Pascal echoed the same truth when he said, "There is a God-shaped vacuum in the heart of every man which cannot be filled by created things, but only by God the Creator made known through Jesus Christ."

It seems that mankind has an eternal heartache that can be filled with nothing less than God. The pleasure of the moment, the delights of life—nothing can fill the God-shaped vacuum tucked away in a restless heart.

If you are lonely, rest securely in God's mighty arms.

If you are drifting, moor your heart in God's Word.

And be prepared for some frosting on an angel food cake.

It's a Giving Time

It was nearing the Christmas season, and Mommie was busy with a hundred things.

The snowflakes for the dining-room window had been cut out and pasted in place. (It was the only "snow" there was last year and the children enjoyed it.) . . .

The fruitcakes were ripening in their tin boxes with a bit of apple in each.

The date bars and nut rolls were snowy white with the powdered sugar Mommie had saved all fall. . . .

The children hugged themselves and each other while squealing in joyous anticipation. The older three told the four babies all the things in store. "And there will be presents—all kinds of pretty packages with dolls and toys and books and engines and maybe even a wind-up train or a kitten."

And then one day it was nearly Christmas. At lunch Mommie was alone with the seven children. "Let's talk about Christmas some more," she said. "We've been talking a lot about what we are going to get . . . what people are going to give to us. But you know, Christmas is more of *giving* than getting. The dear Lord Jesus was God's gift to us and we are so thankful for Him. We like to think of what we can give Him on His birthday."

" . . . our hearts . . . and our love . . . and we can say 'thank you' and 'happy birthday'!" they chorused.

"Yes, and we can also think of others on that day, too. It's a giving time mostly." . . .

It was nearly midnight on Christmas eve before that last white ruffle and blue bow were sewed onto the pink wicker doll-cradle for Jane. As Mommie sat at the dining-room table and sewed in a silence broken only by the noise of the babies turning in their cribs, she thought of the real meaning of Christmas. Not what we are going to get, not even what we have to give, but rather—love to Him and thankfulness for all He gave to us.

We can bring our gifts to Him . . . ourselves, our devotion, and our love. Also our gold and silver, that His work may be carried on and the knowledge of the Lord increased.

It was midnight when the last stitch was taken and the last package wrapped. Daddy came in from the study and together they remembered . . . "It came upon a midnight clear, that glorious song of old . . ." There seemed to be a sense of His nearness and love as they prayed together before going upstairs. He seemed very near and very dear and their hearts were warmed. Do you suppose if they'd had the right kind of ears that they could have heard the angels singing once again at midnight?

I well remember the flurry of activity, often lasting weeks, that surrounded the Christmas holidays. There were fruitcakes to make, cookies to bake, and date bars and nut rolls to assemble and powder with white, wartime-rationed sugar.

Perhaps by necessity, but more likely by choice, Mom was an excellent model of what it means to be a giving, considerate person. Periodically we youngsters would overhear discussions about Mom's need for a new pair of shoes or a piece of clothing. Yet, invariably she would accept what she already knew was inevitable—she wore the coat another year, she had the shoes resoled. The kids' needs always came first.

Yet Mother's life was one of great joy, because she lived what she claimed: "It is better to give than to receive."

The Slippery Slope of Sin

I t happened over a year ago. . .

It was a warm sunny day. The two-year-old twins were barefooted and dressed in fresh, clean sunsuits. Mommie was upstairs bathing the baby; Daddy was out in the study. The older children were playing in the orchard, and the twins were supposedly building blocks in the cool living-room.

Suddenly Mommie heard a thud, a silence, and then another thud. She listened, trying to quiet the baby's splashing in the tub. Thud! Thud! and then angry cries from the twins.

She hastily dried Annette and rolled her in a big towel. Catching up the fluffy white cocoon she hurried down the stairs and out to the kitchen, directed by the thuds and cries.

And there they were, Timmie and Virginia, slipping and falling in a pool of broken eggs. (There had been a dozen of them on the shelf!)

Every time they tried to stand up their bare knees, feet, and hands slid out from under them. From their blond curly heads to their fat pink feet they were well-coated with egg and needed only the rolled cracker crumbs to qualify as veal cutlets! And they were full of rage as well.

It didn't feel funny then. Mommie had just bathed one baby and there were clothes to be put out and dishes to do. She shifted the baby to one arm and phoned out to the study for Daddy to come in. He came and looked and roared with laughter. The twins slipped and flopped and screamed.

"If you think it is so funny, you can clean them up," and Mommie hurried upstairs to slip Net-Net into a nightie and bed. "But Honey," he shouted after her, "Don't you see?—It's just like the wicked to get in slippery places. They got themselves into a mess, and they can't get out by their own efforts."

Mommie wondered briefly why she hadn't married something less theological and hurried back downstairs again.

"You see it's only when someone greater than they can pick them out of the situation that they can be released." He chuckled, picking up a twin by the hands and feet and starting through the house and up the stairs. "Don't drip egg all over the rugs," answered Mommie, following along with the other twin held the same way.

"And you see, they have to be cleaned up, and not by their own efforts," added Daddy as he dropped twin plus sunsuit into Annette's bathwater.

Mother remarked that she thought that by now she had grasped the point sufficiently well. She avoided the twinkle in Daddy's eye lest an answering one kindle in her's.

She left Daddy to digest the points he had so clearly expounded (and to bathe and shampoo the twins). She walked through the kitchen, carefully skirting the pool of eggs which she left for Daddy to clean up as long as he enjoyed it so!

It was sunny in the clothes-yard but there was a cool breeze. She was almost tempted to chuckle a bit, but remembered her wrath in time. "Anyway, it *was* like the wicked. Those twins stole the eggs and then were caught in the results of their own sin and were powerless to escape. It illustrates a point all right," thought Mommie. "But what an illustration!"

A THOUGHT FROM JOE

In this teachable moment there is another thing to learn from this dynamic duo and their scrambled omelette—that wherever you go, whatever you do, whatever you become . . . your Heavenly Father is there, "looking down in tender love." Yes, He loves us even when we spill our milk or break the eggs.

So much so that He sent His only Son to solve the demands
of divine holiness so that we could become sons and
daughters of the King. All hail King Jesus! . . . And thanks
for keeping an eye on us.

Becky had been naughty, and now in the quiet of her room she was tearfully repentant. Mommie went in and sat on the edge of bed. It was dark, but the light from the hallway streamed across the rug. She sat there holding Becky's hand, wondering what to say. Perhaps a little bit of

Love in God's Face

loving was now the most needed thing. (And the bouncy little four-year-old was not hard to love with her hair just growing into pigtail length and a button of a nose that wrinkled when she laughed.)

Becky's arms reached up to pull Mommie down to the pillow. There were several quick hugs, one last sob, and a sigh of satisfaction.

"Let me see your face, Mommie. Put on the light; I want to see your face." And so Mother reached over and switched on the light. Becky looked carefully and then smiled and wriggled all over. The love she saw there—and "nothing between," satisfied her heart. She had known that she was forgiven, but she had to see it in Mommie's face.

We, too, have known the joy of forgiveness. Time and time again we have come to the Lord to have things made

(Con't)

right. He has forgiven us, that we know, for "if we confess our sins, He is faithful and just to forgive us our sins, and to cleanse us from all unrighteousness" (1 John1:9).

With the eye of faith we look into His face and know that nothing stands between us. But someday, oh joyous thought, SOMEDAY we shall see Him face to face! Our eyes shall behold Him, and our hearts will be full to overflowing as we realize the inexpressible love revealed in His face. . . .

Mommie tucked Becky in, turned and smoothed her pillow, and closed the door softly after one backward glance at the chubby little repentant all cuddled down to sleep— satisfied.

A THOUGHT FROM JOE

Jesus catches up with you as you are hiking along the shore of a beautiful lake. He puts his arm around you and looks you in the eye. Tell me about His face. Describe it. Is there a smile or a frown, gentleness or anger? What would He say to you? What might He do for you? What would you say to Him as He tells you, "You are forgiven—and greatly loved"?

Let God Choose

Jon stopped a minute to talk with Mommie, who was washing the dishes. He leaned in the doorway and suddenly asked. "Do you think I'll ever be a famous 'imposer'?"

Mother eyed him speculatively. "You are right *now*, you little rascal," she chuckled to herself, and then said to her seven-year-old, "What *composer* do you have in mind, son?"

"Well . . . there was a little boy . . . I forget his name. Our teacher told us. He was only four, and he could play wonderful. And the king heard him and asked him to play. And he sent him some clothes to play in. So the little boy went to his palace, and he slipped on the slippery floor, like our gym, and the little princess—she was eight—picked him up and he said, 'Someday I'm going to marry you'". . . .

Mommie broke in with, "Was the composer you're thinking of named Liszt, Mendelssohn, or Beethoven?"

"His father's name was Beethoven. That's what Miss Lewis said."

"Perhaps you will be a famous man someday, sonny," Mommie suggested. "But the best thing to do is to let the Lord decide for you.". . .

Mommie remembered another conversation she and Jon had one night after bedtime prayer together. "How do you ever decide what you're going to be when you grow up?" he had asked.

And then in the next sentence he answered his own question. "I'm going to let the Lord pick me out what He wants me to be."

Mommie looked at him all clean and sweet and quiet in bed, so different from his grubby, noisy daytime self. She sent up a quick prayer, "Oh, Lord *keep him this way with his heart soft toward Thee. Make it real in his life.*"

What can mothers and fathers do these days when every child is beset by every form of temptation? Only this . . . pray, counsel, and guide under the leadership of the Lord. For was it not said of Him, "You will show me the path of life; in Your presence is fullness of joy; at Your right hand are pleasures for evermore" Psalm 16:ll? So for us all, not just for Jon, is the privilege of saying, "*I'm going to let the Lord pick me out what He wants me to be.*"

A verse learned around the table shaped much of my life and thoughts about the future. "Commit you way unto the Lord, and He will give you the desires of your heart." As I daily commit my way to Him, as I review my schedule with Him, as I invite God's kingdom to reign in my life, I'm changed. I want His way at any cost. His way is perfect, and this very perfection reminds me of the folly of rejecting it. In surrendering to His plans, my plans change and my priorities are adjusted.

When I surrender my ways and embrace His ways, He gives me the desires of my renewed heart.

'Tis far, far better to let Him choose

The way that we should take;

If only we leave our life with Him

He will guide without mistake.

We, in our blindness, would never choose

A pathway dark and rough,

And so we should ever find in Him,

"The God who is enough."

ANONYMOUS

Here are a couple of Mother's recipes for you to enjoy.

GINGERSNAPS

1 cup molasses

1/2 cup shortening

1/2 cup butter

3 1/2 cups flour

1/4 teaspoon baking soda

1 tablespoon ginger

1 teaspoon cinnamon

1/4 teaspoon ground cloves

1 1/4 teaspoon salt

Heat molasses to boiling. Pour it over the shortening and butter. Sift the dry ingredients and stir into the molasses mixture. Mix well and let rest in the refrigerator for about 20 minutes. Roll the dough out in small batches as thin as possible and cut into heart shapes. Bake at 350 degrees for 8 to 10 minutes. This recipe will make about 5 dozen cookies, depending upon the size of your cookie cutter.

CHRISTMAS DATE BARS

1 1/4 cups chopped dates

1 1/4 cups chopped pecans

3 teaspoons baking powder

3 eggs (not beaten)

3 tablespoons flour (yes, tablespoons not cups!)

1 1/4 cups powdered sugar, plus additional amount for
   rolling the bars in after baking

Grease an 8 x 13 pan. In a large bowl mix the ingredients
in the order given. Do not overmix. Spread the mixture in the
greased pan and bake at 375 degrees for 30 minutes. While
still warm, cut into bars and roll in powdered sugar. These are
chewy and delicious!